Shopify Guide 2020

A Step-by-Step Guide for Beginners-
Make Money from Shopify:
Create A Store, Drop Shipping
Store Management & Marketing

Jessica Ker

Table of Contents

Introduction

Shopify is a platform that you can create your own online store. You can do drop shipping and affiliate marketing with your Shopify store.

In this book, we will show you a step-by-step guide to how to create a store, how to manage your store, marketing your products and do affiliate marketing. You will get a free Checklist at the end of the book, it will help you start from zero to one.

Here is what you will learn from this book:

- How to find the most profitable niche to start
- A step-by-step guide to create a store, including choose domain, install theme, website customization etc.
- The channels for marketing your products.
- Recommend tools for keywords research, store management and data analytics.
- Techniques get ranking on search engines
- How to source products from China
- How to do SEO for your Shopify store

Here is our All-in-One Free Resource for Shopify business. Please check our website: **www.sinogrows.com**

If you have any questions, you can reach out us on **Facebook group**.
https://www.facebook.com/groups/65025056553013 0/

Happy Learning!

Chapter 1: Understanding Drop shipping business

1.1 What is Drop shipping?

Drop shipping is an order fulfillment model that a business company or individual don't keep products in stock. When the sellers receive orders, they order products from a third-party supplier, who then ships the order to the customer. The third-party can be a wholesaler or an eCommerce store. The drop shipper doesn't directly handle the products, but they can track the shipment.

1.2 How to do drop shipping with Shopify store?

It works in 4 steps:

Your customers place orders on your Shopify Store.

1) You buy products from your suppliers on AliExpress, eBay or other countries.

2) Suppliers ship the products to your customers directly. They gave you the track number when they delivered the products.

3) Your customers received the products.

There are two different types dropshipping model:

One is sourcing products that you can find one big eCommerce platforms, such as AliExpress, Alibaba, Salehoo,eBay etc.

Another is POD (Print on Demand), that means when your customers want customized products, such as T-shirt,mug, posters etc, you can use POD websites, such as Printify, Zazzle, TeeSpring etc. This is similar as the first one, but your customers can buy customized products.

1.3 Make money from affiliate marketing with your store?

Besides the drop-shipping models, you can also do affiliate marketing with your store.

Affiliate marketing is a performance-based marketing program. It is promoting and referring products or services by other companies or individuals to your audience, and earn a commission when getting sales. The sales are tracked by affiliate links from your Shopify website.

How does this work?

The overall goal of an affiliate program creates a win-win system for both companies and partners. Let's see how it works. You provide a product or service of other companies. And link it to your Shopify store, so your customers can purchase the product or service.

The link here is the key. It's called an "affiliate link." This link is unique to all of their affiliates, and it is how merchants (companies or individuals) to track the referral. The merchants will provide you with a unique link when you sign up and apply to be an affiliate.

If someone clicks on the affiliate link, a cookie is placed on their browser, and if they make a purchase, the merchant knows it to reward you for the referral.

When you get the link, you can place it in a different place and link it to the relevant posts when your customers can get a purchase.

How to Apply to be An Affiliate?

There are two primary choices to partner with affiliates: for an individual company or an affiliate network. we recommend doing both of them.

Let's talk about the difference between them.

When sign up with an individual company will allow you to promote their company's products or services. After signing up once, you can then promote specific products or the company as a whole.

If signing up with an affiliate network, on the other hand, this means you can become an affiliate for any of the companies or personal brands that the network represents.

They will have a list of their partners on the website. For example, affiliate networks like ShareASale or Clickbank let you search for and sign up with any of the companies they represent.

Some affiliate programs and networks may require a simple application process to ensure they're only partnering with high-quality websites. But most of them don't care about your site's traffic, as long as you regularly get great posts to your blog site.

No matter what you choose, you sign up with an individual company or affiliate network, or both of them, it's crucial that you keep your standards high.

I recommend only promoting some products or companies you have personal experience with and would recommend to friends, family, and your audience.

If you want to start with affiliate networks, here are some of the most popular ones:

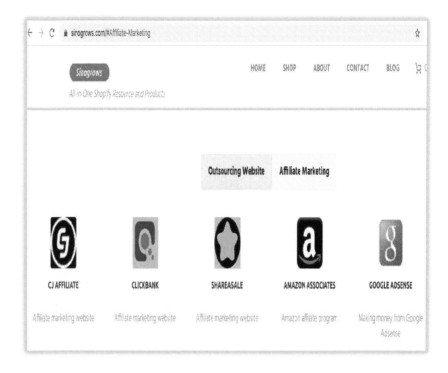

Affiliate Networks List

Amazon Associates: Although Amazon offers very low commission rates, it's also the most straightforward program to use. Signing up with Amazon is easy, and because they provide a large number of products, you can easily find the products that attract your audience. And the more products you sell, the higher your commission rate is!

CJ Affiliate: It's known as Commission Junction. It's one of the largest affiliate marketing networks.

ShareASale: offering different category products and services, such as home& garden, fashion, business, and so on.

Clickbank: Specializes in digital products, such as language course, Forex, software, and so on. Digital products give you higher commissions than for tangible goods – sometimes, the commissions even run as high as 80-90%!

You can check the commission before promoting it.

E-junkie: Another network specializes in digital products like eBooks, comics, art, music, video, and software. These can even offer up to a 100% commission for digital products!

Rakuten Affiliate Network: This company acquired LinkShare LinkShare. It's one of the largest pay-for-performance affiliate marketing networks.

*Keep in mind that you need to sign up for a free affiliate account before you can see a full list of stores or businesses that participate in each network.

Summary: Here's the entire affiliate marketing process:

1) You apply to be an affiliate.
2) Merchant or networks approve your application. The merchant or network provides you with unique affiliate links and relevant materials for promotion.
3) You create products on your store and add the affiliate links to the affiliate products within your Shopify store.
4) You promote the products you added on your store, such as social media marketing, video marketing, and so on.
5) A potential consumer clicks on the link, when the interested consumer makes an order within the cookie lifespan, the merchant identifies the affiliate based on the unique identifier based on the cookie. You need not

worry about this part because the merchant's affiliate program software takes care of this.

6) Then You will earn a commission based on a pre-determined rate. Eventually, you will make big money on it

1.4 Why do you start the Shopify business?

Drop shipping is effectively taking out the process of having deliveries from suppliers to your company first and instead, merely getting them to deliver the product directly to the customer. It cuts out the unnecessary steps of receiving orders, storing, packing the products, and providing the items. The Drop shipping saves money on postage, storage space, stock, the workforce needed to process the orders.

Following are six strong reasons why you should start the Drop shipping:

1.Low cost to get started

It needs only a small capital to start the business. You don't need to invest a lot of money to keep stock. In other words, you don't buy anything that you haven't sold. And you can sell products with little money. All you need is choosing a proper channel and some tools to start your Drop shipping business.

2.Broad Range Products to Sell

Different from brick and mortar shops, the Drop shipping business allows you to choose various products to sell on your online store. And there are lots of suppliers and brands which you can select. You don't need to worry about the space for stocking your products.

You can pick products from various niches. Whether you're interested in cosmetics, healthy products, baby's products, toys, or automobiles, there's always the right niche for you. And you can test different options based on your research.

Meanwhile, you can sell bundles or bulk products without keeping inventory. You will have more chances to reach more consumers.

3.Work from anywhere, anytime.

A drop shipper can operate from all over the world, ship items from suppliers in China, and deliver to customers to any other countries without moving an inch, just by a few clicks.

If you love traveling, independent, or working remotely, then drop shipping should be on your to-do list.

4.Automation Your Business

If you get all the work done manually, it would be a real hassle.

Some useful tools can help you with automation. Automation makes drop shipping even more straightforward and quicker than you can imagine. For instance, you can use some tools like Oberlo for automating the drop shipping process, so you can focus on working on the store marketing.

With automation, you can avoid some mistakes, such as inventory or pricing mistakes, you save time, money, and improve efficiency.

5.Different Channels to Choose

A sales channel is a platform that you sell your products.

There are plenty of options out there, and there are four popular sales platforms: Amazon, eBay, AliExpress, and your eCommerce store, like Shopify.

Of course, you can use multiple platforms if you want.

6. Online Shopping Growth

According to Statista, the report shows that an estimated 1.8 billion people worldwide purchase goods online in 2018. During the same year, global e-retail sales amounted to 2.8 trillion U.S. dollars. The estimated amount will be up to 4.8 trillion U.S. dollars by 2021.

According to Invesp, the countries with the leading average eCommerce revenue per shoppers are: USA ($1,804), UK ($1,629), Sweden ($1,446), France ($1,228), Germany ($1,064), Japan ($968), Spain ($849), China ($626), Russia ($396), and Brazil ($350).

There are some advantages and disadvantages of Drop shipping.

Advantages:

- No inventory.

You don't have any inventory pressure. When customers order products in your store, you can contact the supplier and ask the supplier to ship the items directly. In this way, there is no problem with the backlog of goods, which dramatically reduces the risk of operations. Moreover, the selected product will surely have sufficient inventory guarantees, and there will be no problem of being unable to trade due to a lack of goods.

- A wide range of products.

Without the limitations of space cost, a drop shipper is flexible to offer the customers with more choices. It allows retailers to have a vast, ever-changing inventory that gets more sales income.

Not only the variety of goods is complete, but also the style is vibrant and colorful, you can adjust the product style and type according to market demand, which significantly enhances the competitiveness of the store.

- Much quicker to get products to the market

Usually, a seller wants to start selling a product, and they'll have to wait until the products to be shipped to the warehouse. But using drop shipping means that when you decide you want a product on your site, you can start advertising almost immediately. The product can come to the market as quickly as possible.

If you want to test the potential of new products, it will be at low risk and low cost.

- Flexibility

The drop shipping model offers flexibility that would not be possible without it. The drop shipper can run the business anywhere and anytime as long as they have an Internet connection. With the Internet, buyers can directly communicate with manufacturers or store owners at the same time with customers.

It gives flexibility to merchants since they can partner with multiple wholesale suppliers and sell more products to their customers. Manufacturers also get more flexibility since there is more product movement.

- Leverage

In business, being able to multiply your money, time, and an effort is a form of leverage. By offering drop shipping to wholesale customers, you'll be able to prioritize on establishing relationships with these buyers.

Having reliable and dependable dropship wholesalers who will do the shipping for you balances the burden between the merchant and the supplier.

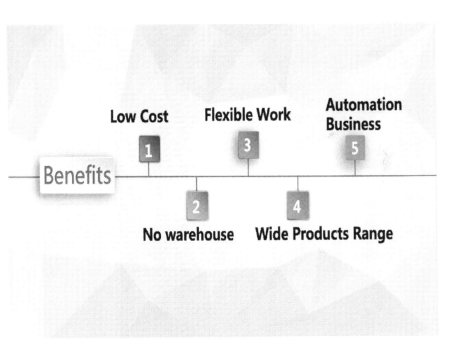

- Saving time

Organizing your stock and preparing it for delivery is a time-consuming task. Using a third-party to ship items, like printing, labeling, packing, shipment, can save you a lot of time. This gives you more free time to focus on growing your business in marketing and other vital factors.

Drop shipping sounds like the easiest and ideal business. With no significant upfront investment required, it's an appealing option for many people who want to make money. But there are still some disadvantages out there.

- Less competitive pricing

Drop shipping means no more bulk pricing. You might pay more for each item when drop shipping, so that means your prices won't be as competitive.

When you drop-ship items, you will be paying $3 more each product compared to sellers who purchase in large quantities. This may make it difficult to compete on eCommerce like eBay, especially if you are selling hot-sale products.

- Less control

The products you are selling rely on the stock of your supplier. Sudden stock shortages will affect your sales. You might discover that the product you sell is out of stock. It happens if you use Drop Shipping on eBay or Amazon, and your customers will be frustrated if they had purchased a product that is not available. To eliminate this problem, you can use an automated tool that updates stock availability regularly. You can request a notice or email from the supplier if the stock has run out.

When you use third-party logistics, sometimes it will be out of control. If the drop shipper makes an error and leaves your customer displeased, that reflects on your business. So, it's essential to work with reliable suppliers and logistic companies.

- Customer service issue If you are selling various products, you are not familiar with the products and not having all the product details, so you might not answer customer inquiries about the products' dimensions, weight, ease of use, packing, and so on. Lack of product information and real experience of the product may mean you can provide less useful and unique content on your store, which also affects the sales conversion.

- High competition

Finding great drop shipping products will often mean you will face more top competition from fellow retailers in your sector. The margins of drop shipping products can be quite low as many manufacturers charge for the fulfillment service, so you may have a little margin to maneuver your prices to beat your competitors.

Summary:

Drop shipping is a fantastic way to sell items online store, and you just need to make sure that you can source a reliable supplier and get a competitive price. Selling on the right channels, you select and making money from Drop shipping.

Affiliate marketing is a good choice for Shopify store, or you would combine both the drop shipping and affiliate marketing in one store. It is flexible business. You will need to find the best way to make money in your niche.

Chapter 2: How to select a profitable niche ?

There are a lot of products categories out there, how to find a profitable niche for your business is very critical.

Maybe some people recommend you to go for something that matches your interests. But you shouldn't just pick the products you like the most. It will be better if the products you are interested in are the right decision after your research. It gives you more interest in doing long business time. We strongly recommend you to choose your products with market research if you want to create a profitable drop shipping store. Because products are vital to the success of your drop shipping business. For that reason, consider your options carefully.

Choosing the best drop shipping niche for your store can be broken into three broad steps: Brainstorming your ideas, using *Methods & Recommend Tools to validate the success*, and make a decision.

Step 1: Brainstorming Your Ideas

Before you drive in the drop shipping business and test different niches for profitability, you need to think of the possible niches you might do. This means you need to focus on brainstorming your ideas and make a list of all your ideas.

Don't limit your ideas. Create a list that comes up with wild ideas and generate as many ideas as possible. Start the brainstorming with some questions:

- What products did you buy online?
- What do people like to buy when traveling?
- What are the hobbies of your family?
- What's the most expensive thing you bought before?

Group brainstorming can be productive, and you may ask your family or your friends to talk about them. The group encourages divergent thinking and enhances the quality of thought and decisions.

Step 2: *Success Validation--Methods & Recommend Tools*

While you have finished the list of brainstorming ideas, you will need to validate the success of the ideas. You can use different methods and tools to do this.

- Use AliExpress to find a niche

AliExpress is a B2C marketplace based in China, present in more than 190 countries and regions. It's founded in 2010 and owned by Alibaba Group. AliExpress has more than 150 million users.

You can use AliExpress to find a niche for your store. The relevant statistics that help you understand if you can find potential customers for the products of your niche.

There are some data you may check:

First, the number of AliExpress products in your niche.

We check the number of items that can be found on AliExpress when you search for a specific keyword. The volume is more than 100 items. We include only the products that have free shipping with a four or 5-star rating.

Second: The popularity and feedbacks of the product niche.

Check the orders of on the first page, try to figure out the following answers to the questions:

- How long has the store been set up?
- What's the feedback score of the products?
- How many average orders per month?
- What's the score of the shipping speed?

Finding a niche on Facebook Groups

Facebook is one of the most popular marketing platforms to reach your audience all over the world. It founded in 2004 by Mark Zuckerberg.

Facebook Demographics:

The monthly active users of Facebook are 2.45 billion at the end of 2019.

The average Facebook user has 155 friends.

84% of users are among 30-49-year-old.

Around 69% of users are US adults.

The number of active mobile users is 2.26 billion.

43% of users are female, 57% male.

The users created their personal profile on Facebook, and we can target based on their details, such as demographics, job title, the age of a user's kids, their location, the hobbies, their activities, etc.

Groups are a certain number of people with shared interests.

Enter a keyword in the search box, click the 'Groups' tab on Facebook. You will see a list of Facebook groups, and you can view the number of their members. We may consider a niche to be prospective if it has more than 15 groups with more than 30,000 members in each group.

Using Google Trends to choose the niche

Google Trends is a free online tool provided by Google. The data of Google trends shows the search volume of the keywords in target countries and language.

Downloading the data and charting the data in a spreadsheet, you will see the different search trends in different seasons and relevant keywords within your niche.

Use Amazon to choose the niche

Amazon is one of the biggest international eCommerce retailers, and it sells more than 12 million products online. Over 95 million people have Amazon Prime members in the US.

There are three steps to find a profitable niche and products for your drop shipping business.

Step one: check the best seller category which you have chosen. Better to find the high demand products with little competition.

Step two: narrow down the niche. You can check the "sub-niche' on the left-hand side of the best seller pages.

Step three: check the reviews of the products.

- Using Jungle Scout

Jungle Scout is an excellent software to find your products, and the price starts at $19 each month. You can quickly filter out the products by review counts, average sales, and category.

Select Profitable Products

- AliExpress
- eBay
- Facebook
- Google Trends
- Amazon
- Jungle Scout

Drop shipping niche to avoid:

Some specific niches should be approached with great caution. We recommend you think carefully if you want to sell them in your online store.

- Large and heavy products

Price is one of the most critical aspects. People usually purchase cheap products without thinking.

Because the large and heavy product is weight more, the shipping will be more. Most people don't want to spend more on transportation.

According to e-commerce statistics, an average of 30% of US online shoppers canceled their orders because of the high shipping cost.

- Items that can easily get damaged during transportation

Because fragile items broken is one of the biggest mistakes drop shippers make, and which reduces their chances of generating return sales. Fragile items are susceptible to damage during the shipment. Such as ceramics and glass products.

- Copyright/Trademark Products

The United States trademark stated that using someone else's logo without permission, even if it's unregistered, is against the law.

You will probably get into a legal issue if you have been selling counterfeits of other brands.

Of course, you can sell the products if you get a license from that company to sell these products officially.

A copyrighted product is a product that has been copied from other brands. You can't add these products to your online store, such as Nike sneaker shoes, Chanel products, etc.

These are some products that you cannot sell:

- **Unregulated supplements**
- **Used products (cosmetics, underwear, etc.)**
- **Third-Party infringements**
- **Surveillance equipment**
- **Counterfeit products**
- **Health products: "Before-and-After."**
- **Controversial products**
- **Firearms, weapons**
- **Tobacco products**
- **Human remains and body parts**
- **Drugs and drug-related products**
- **Other illegal products**

If you want to use the Amazon ads to do the marketing, you may check the Facebook ads here: https://www.facebook.com/policies/ads. There is a list of products you can't do ads on Amazon.

- Dangerous product

Many countries have stringent restrictions on the products forbidden to sell. You may need to research to figure out about these restrictions.

Step 3: Action -Making a decision

Now you've done a validation process for the niche that you had listed. You should have a clear idea about the market size, your competitors, and monetization potential for each niche. So, decide to narrow down your niches.

You need to trust yourself; you will get succeed in drop shipping. A winning mindset will ensure you are not afraid to fail. When you fail, you learn. Every mistake you made can be adapted and thus applied to your next venture. A proper mindset will mean you view failure as an opportunity for success. You should not be afraid to spend money on Facebook advertising. Drop shipping is inexpensive to begin, but you must be willing to part with some cash. View this as a learning experience. You are collecting valuable data to allow your Facebook pixel to optimize and target the perfect customer. You will find the right people for your store. Spending money will increase the likelihood that you find these people.

Useful tips for picking the niche:

Products with high-quality photos

High-quality photos are one of the most critical factors for drop shipping. It can only show the looks of the product, but also makes it unique. You can get the free stock photos that your supplier provides, or you can buy some samples, then hire a photographer to take professional photos. Another choice is sourcing another supplier with higher quality images of the same product.

Sell Products Can Get Repeat Orders
Make sure the niche products you're selling can get repeat orders in the future. Consumable goods like skincare products are ideal for repeat business because they need to be replenished over time.

If you provide customers with an excellent product to meet their needs and hobbies, they'll continue returning to your store again.
Create Unique Value

Drop shipping business is competitive because it's easier to get started but how to stand out among the competitors? Several other drop shipping stores will surely offer lower price products that you sell, how does a customer choose your store over others?

You need to provide products or services with a unique value proposition. This means you offer something that better solves your customers' pain points and meets your customers' needs. There are many ways to provide unique value, so don't be afraid to get creative. Come up with the added value that's original and unique to your store.

Conclusion:

You may need to do some research first before you make a decision, check your competitors in your niche and find the most profitable products for your Shopify store.

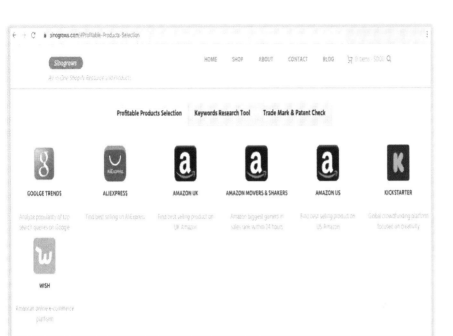

Profitable Products Selection   **Keywords Research Tool**   **Trade Mark & Patent Check**

GOOLGE TRENDS	ALIEXPRESS	AMAZON UK	AMAZON MOVERS & SHAKERS	AMAZON US	KICKSTARTER
Analyze popularity of top search queries on Google	Find best selling on AliExpress	Find best selling product on UK Amazon	Amazon biggest gainers in sales rank within 24 hours	Find best selling product on US Amazon	Global crowdfunding platform focused on creativity

WISH

American online e-commerce platform

Chapter 3: Three Steps to Building Shopify Store

You may hear the Shopify before and a lot of Shopify pro. Do you know what's Shopify? Is Shopify legit? Is Shopify free?

Shopify is a Canadian eCommerce platform, providing services for creating website for selling online. It's legit, but not free. Many people use Shopify to build drop shipping sites to make money online from home. It's one of the great ways to make money on Shopify.

Shopify offers free trial, you can sign up for free Shopify trial. You will need to learn how to do your Shopify website building, sell in Shopify and how to use Shopify for making profit.

Here is a free Shopify tutorial for setting up a Shopify store, only 3 simple steps:

Things you need to do before start:

☐ Store name

☐ Your Shopify logo

☐ Email and address for sign up

☐ Credit Card or PayPal account

☐ Products + pictures + pricing + inventory

Step 1: Shopify Store Set Up

Step 2: Choose a catchy theme & customized your store

Step 3: Choose Shopify plan & payment gateway

Things you need to do before start:

How to name your business is a start. You may use the Shopify name generator to choose name for business. Here is the link: https://www.shopify.com/tools/business-name-generator

What's domain meaning?
Domain definition is that domain name is the address on the internet. It's unique.

Another way is using the domain providers to get the domain search and check the domain availability, and then come up with a business name:

> https://www.instantdomainsearch.com/domain/generator/
> https://www.godaddy.com
> https://www.namecheap.com/
> https://www.hostpapa.com/domains/

You may buy the domain on Shopify though a price a little high than you bought from other domain providers.

For the Shopify logo, you can use online free Shopify logo maker, such as Canvas. It's easy to make a stunning logo instantly.

Step 1: Sign up an account on Shopify

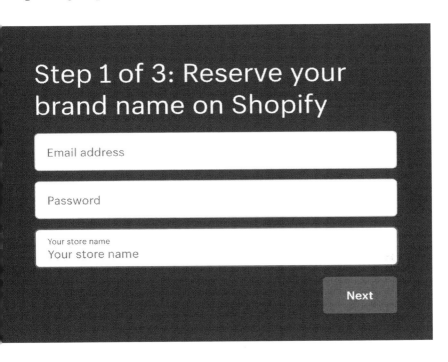

Use your email to register an account, and verify your email address.

You can apply for more than one store on Shopify with the same email address, make sure you turn off the VPN before you start signing up with Shopify. You can sell products all over the world.

When you enter your Shopify site, you can add it to your bookmark this tap. You can
sign in Shopify by one-click.

Understand the Shopify Admin

When you access my Shopify login, you will see the Shopify administration, or panel.

It includes 6 main important sections:

- Order: It allows you create orders and manage all the orders here.
- Products: this if for editing your products and collections, inventory management for Shopify.
- Analytics: check your store data here, including total sales, store conversion, traffic source, social source, etc.,
- Marketing: view your marketing date, including overview, campaigns and automations.
- Sales channels--Online Store: you can edit your theme, posting, pages, menu, footer, header etc.
- Setting: update your store information, setting your payment, shipping, billing, sales channels, location etc.

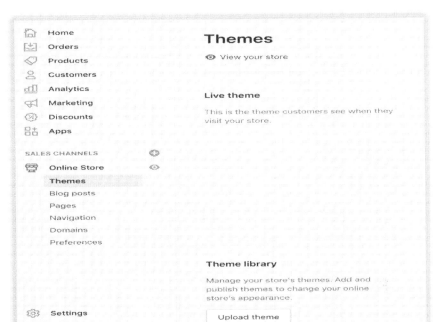

Themes

👁 View your store

Home
Orders
Products
Customers
Analytics
Marketing
Discounts
Apps

SALES CHANNELS

Online Store

Themes
Blog posts
Pages
Navigation
Domains
Preferences

Live theme

This is the theme customers see when they visit your store.

Theme library

Manage your store's themes. Add and publish themes to change your online store's appearance.

Settings

Upload theme

Settings

General View and update your store details	**Locations** Manage the places you stock inventory, fulfil orders, and sell products	**Plan and permissions** View plan information and manage what staff can see or do in your store.
Payment providers Enable and manage your store's payment providers	**Gift cards** Enable Apple Wallet passes and set gift card expiry dates	**Store languages** Manage the languages your customers can view on your store
Checkout Customize your online checkout process	**Notifications** Manage notifications sent to you and your customers	**Billing** Manage your billing information and view your invoices
Shipping Manage how you ship orders to customers	**Files** Upload images, videos, and documents	**Legal** Manage your store's legal pages
Taxes Manage how your store charges taxes	**Sales channels** Manage the channels you use to sell your products and services	

Domain & Email

A good domain is the first step to your branding.

4 Tips to select a perfect domain for your store:

1) Keep it short and easy to read

Long domain name is difficult to remember and not easy to type.

2) Use your keywords

3) Choose .com domain extension

4) Make it unique

In terms of the domain, you may buy it on Shopify or you can buy it from domain providers. If you already bought it from domain provider, you need to connect your existing domain with store. And you will need to point your domain to Shopify.

The price of the domain varies, it depends on the domain name you choose. But ordinary domain costs around $5 each year. You will need to pay the domain at least one year. You may check the price on domain sites, such as GoDaddy, Namecheap, Domain.com etc.

Before you connect your existing domain with Shopify, you will need to change the DNS. Go to the domain provider, change A record and add Shopify IP address. Check the following step images.

Steps:

1. Log in to the account you have with your domain provider.

2. Find your DNS settings. Look for your domain management area, DNS configuration, or similar.

3. Edit your A record to point to Shopify's IP address 23.227.38.65 Copy

   The domain settings panel might feature drop-downs or editable fields, or you might have to check boxes or edit a table. You need to:

   - enter or choose the @ symbol, or **A record**
   - enter Shopify's IP address 23.227.38.65 Copy as the destination for the A record.

4. Save the A Record (click **Save, Save Zone File, Add Record**, or similar).

5. Find the CNAME record in your DNS settings.

6. Change your www CNAME record to point to shops.myshopify.com Copy. Often, you need to provide just the prefix without the dot, but for some domain providers you need the whole subdomain. Use the existing entries as a guide, or follow your provider's instructions. CNAME records must always point to a domain name, never to an IP address.

7. Save the CNAME Record (usually by clicking **Save** or **Add record** or similar).

After you point your domain to Shopify, click "connect existing domain", enter the domain you want to connect, and click "verify connection".

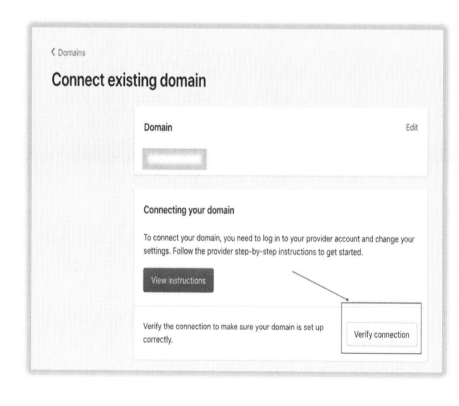

Step 2: Choose a catchy theme & customized your store

☐ Add the theme

You may check some Shopify web examples first, you may search it on Google

site: myshopify.com + (keywords in your niche). It will show all a list of Shopify website examples. Go through these stores, you will know the Shopify storefront examples you like. And you may read some Shopify success story before you start.

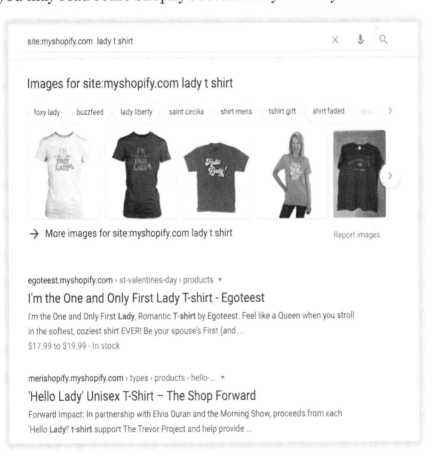

Three ways to get a theme:

1) Shopify free themes

   Click on "Explore free theme", you will see some free Shopify themes. If you have limited budget to start, you may consider choosing the free theme.

2) Shopify paid theme, the price is about US $150.

   Before you buy a theme, we recommend you read these tips:

   - List all the features you want.
   - View the demo site to make sure it has the features you want. It would save your time customize the theme.
   - It's an up-to-date theme.
   - Select a responsive theme. This means the design can be compatible with laptop, iPad, mobile phone etc. It would be easy to use on multiple devices.

3) Upload theme you got from your designer or from the third-party, such as Themeforest.net. The theme there is high-quality with affordable price around US$30. You would download the theme when you bought it. The theme needs to be in ZIP file on Shopify.

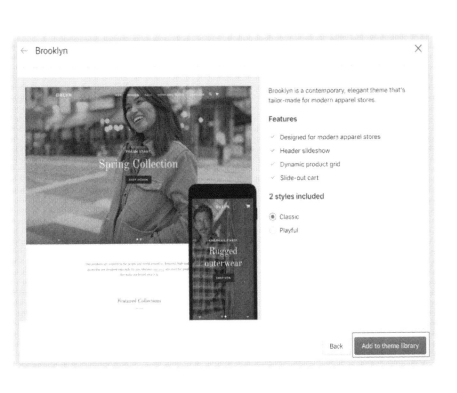

☐ Create main menu, footer & pages

Add the main menu of your store, basically we need "homepage, about us, contact us, shop", you can add the menus you want according to your needs.

Tap the "Navigation", click "Add menu item", you can add the menus in a few minutes.

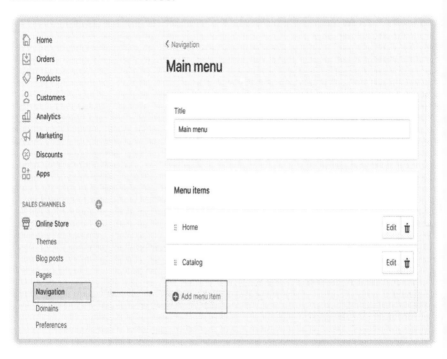

If you want to create a page for "contact us" "about us" or "FAQ", you will need to go to "Online store" --- "pages".

□ Change the logo, pictures

If you want to change the logo, tap the "Online store"—
"Theme"— "Customize"

Also, you can change theme related stuff here, such the theme
text color, background etc.

You can hide the sections if you don't need it. Just click the eye button beside the section.

☐ Create a "Order Track" page

This allows your customers to track their order like this:

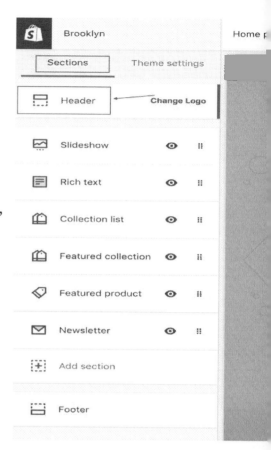

Here are some options here:

Using paid apps, such as Aftership,Shippo.

Free provider: 17 track

Two steps to use the 17 track to do this:

⇒ Click "Online Store"— "Pages" -- "Add Pages"

⇒ Click "Show HTML" button

⇒ Copy & Paste the code I gave below and "Save" it.

⇒

Code: (copy and paste all the following codes marked in Italic below and the next page)

<! --Tracking number input box. -->

<input type="text" id="YQNum" maxlength="50"/>

<!--The button is used to call script method.-->

<input type="button" value="TRACK" onclick="doTrack()"/>

<!--Container to display the tracking result.-->

<div id="YQContainer"></div>

<!--Script code can be put in the bottom of the page, wait until the page is loaded then execute.-->

```
<script type="text/javascript"
src="//www.17track.net/externalcall.js"></script>
<script type="text/javascript">
function doTrack() {
    var num = document.getElementById("YQNum").value;
    if(num===""){
        alert("Enter your number.");
        return;
    }
    YQV5.trackSingle({
        //Required, Specify the container ID of the carrier
content.
        YQ_ContainerId:"YQContainer",
        //Optional, specify tracking result height, max height
800px, default is 560px.
        YQ_Height:560,
        //Optional, select carrier, default to auto identify.
        YQ_Fc:"0",
        //Optional, specify UI language, default language is
automatically detected based on the browser settings.
        YQ_Lang:"en",
        //Required, specify the number needed to be tracked.
        YQ_Num:num
    });
}
</script>
```

☐ Create "Return Policy", "Privacy Policy", "Term of Service", and "Shipping policy".

You use create from the template offered by Shopify privacy policy generator on your dashboard, just click "setting" at the left bottom side— "legal"— "create from template", you will see the screenshots below.

Check the privacy policy example and other example first, make some change when necessary.

Then you will get all the Shopify privacy policy, term of service, shipping policy done.

Or you can just type "legal" on the dashboard search bar.

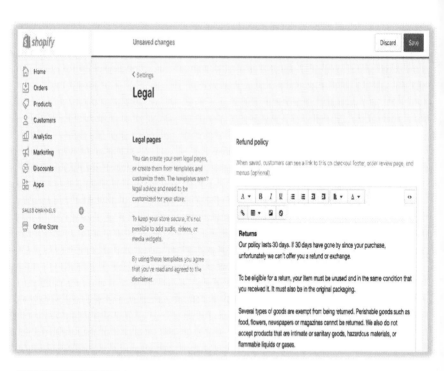

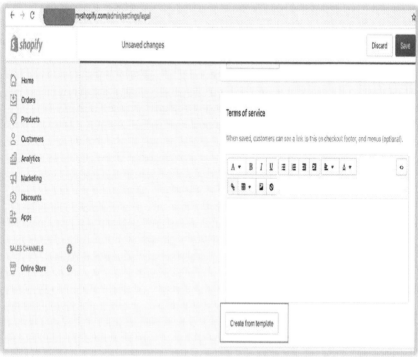

☐ Upload products, picture, price, inventory

If you buy products from AliExpress, you may use the Oberlo to upload the products.
AliExpress is an eCommerce site owned by Alibaba group, you can buy products at low MOQ at low price. MOQ meaning minimum order quantity, you can order 1 product from Chinese seller. And then you resell it to your customer.

What is Oberlo?

Oberlo is an application owned by Shopify, it allows sellers to import products from suppliers to Shopify store and ship to your customers. Just few clicks you can upload the products from Oberlo to Shopify. It offers free Oberlo Chrome extension too.
Here is the process of using Oberlo:

Be sure that you provide the informational products with high-quality images.

1) Sign up a free account on Oberlo with your email address, and get Oberlo login in.

2) Connect your Shopify with Oberlo, and add your store domain

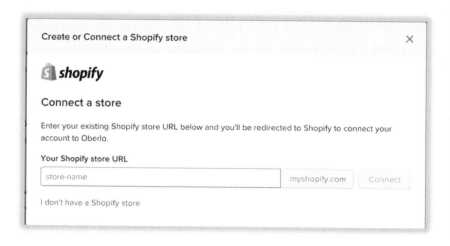

3) Install Oberlo app

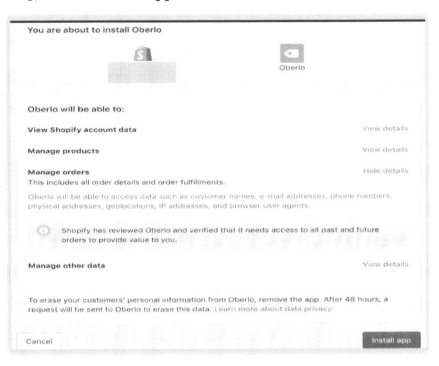

4) Import products from AliExpress & customize all the
   products

If you already found the products on AliExpress, you can add
the products by links or ID. You may need to change the
Shopify pricing, product description etc.

If you don't have it yet, you may click the search, it will access
to AliExpress directly. You can choose products there.

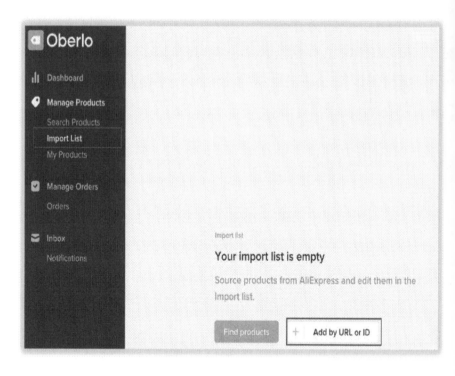

☐ Set up the shipping rate

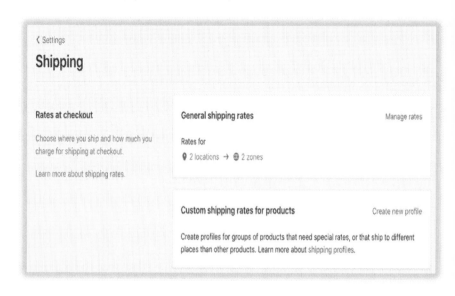

Click on the "manage rate', you may set free shipping or different shipping cost for different countries.

Set Email newsletter
Subscriptions on Shopify is a tool to collect emails for your business.
Easy way to do is choosing the theme which has the sign-up section. You would check the "customers" section on the dashboard, it shows you the email list you corrected.
You may use this to send the promotion, email with Shopify for the future marketing campaign.

Mailchimp for Shopify is a good choice for your email newsletter, you can integrate Mailchimp with Shopify. Shopify Mailchimp can save you time and money for Shopify subscriptions and email automation.

Install Shopify Apps
Shopify apps is similar to website plugs, you can call it Shopify plugin if you like.
Choose some apps or Shopify plugins that can help optimize the process of managing and growing your business.

Here we recommend you install this three free apps:
Dianxiaomi, Free trust badge,

If you source products from AliExpress, you may consider install the "Dianxiaomi", it's a free ERP software. You will easily order from Chinese sellers, keep tracking with your orders, and manage the inventory.

If you want to install the "Dianxiaomi", just click the "Add app" from the Shopify apps store section on your dashboard, then install it, it will directly access to the "Dianmixiao" webpage. You will need to sign up first, then add your store there.

Trust badge
Add Trust badges on your store to increase the conversion, choose a trust badge png and upload to store.
Or you may go to the Shopify apps store to find trust badges to install. It offers some free trust badges, and it would be added to the store footer or the checkout page.

Step 3: How to choose Shopify plans
How much does Shopify cost?
The Shopify cost depends on the Shopify plan you choose. The Shopify pricing range from $29 to $299 per month. The transaction cost is from 2.4% to 2.9%. It offers Shopify plus for large enterprise, the price of Shopify plus stars at $2,000 each month.

There are three Shopify plans: Basic Shopify, Shopify and Advanced Shopify. They have different features, the fees for Shopify. you can select the one suitable for you. Of course, as a startup, you may start with the Basic plan, you can upgrade it to other plans if you need.

If you have Shopify partners, you can set staff accounts for them, so they can use Shopify partners login to the store admin.

You can pay the plan via PayPal or Credit card, also you may select the annual, monthly payment, 2 years or 3 years.

Set up your Shopify payments gateway

Go to the "setting", click on "payment", select the payment way you want. It would be Shopify with PayPal, Shopify with Stripe, Alipay Global etc.

Conclusion:

We already knew how to use Shopify build a website and get drop shipping stores. Now it's time to dive in to keep it up and make money online.

Chapter 4: How to buy from China?

The Ultimate Guide for Purchasing from AliExpress, Alibaba, 1688 &Taobao

How to buy from China?

No matter if you source products for your physical stores or online store, buying from China is an excellent choice. You can import to Vietnam, USA, European countries, or any other countries all over the world.

You can find the manufacturer or wholesale supplier for a wide range of products, such as different types of socks, clothes, bags, fitness equipment, squeeze lip gloss tubes, or white label products etc.

There are 6 channels that you can use for sourcing products directly from China:

1) Alibaba
2) AliExpress
3) DH Gate
4) 1688
5) Taobao
6) Offline marketplaces

Let's get to know more about these six channels, including introduction, platform features, ways to find the suitable supplier, tools for communicating with sellers and protect yourself from buying from suppliers.

4.1 Alibaba

What's Alibaba?

Alibaba belongs to Alibaba group, found in 1999 in Hangzhou city of China. Jacky Ma is one of the founders of Alibaba. It's an B2B marketplace. You can source products in 10 different categories, including Agriculture, Food, Textiles, Sports, Toys, Machinery, Bags, Shoe etc.

Alibaba companies usually sales in bulk, you may get good price if buy in bulk from China.

Not all the suppliers on Alibaba have factory in China, some of them are traders.

1) Is Alibaba legit? Is Alibaba safe?

Yes, Alibaba is legit and it's a safe platform like Amazon. But you will need to check the Alibaba reviews of Alibaba manufacturer before you make an order.

2) How does Alibaba work? How to buy from Alibaba?

Alibaba works similarly as other eCommerce platform.

- You type the keywords or product name on the search bar,
- Select the country you want to source from, and the relate certification you may need to filter the suppliers.
- Make an order.
- The wholesale supplier will arrange shipment from China. You confirm the receiving the goods, the supplier will get the money from Alibaba.

3) How to find suppliers?

Finding the right supplier for your product may take some time, filter the supplier first. Select the supplier type, supplier country, product certification, minimum order quantity etc. Then check with price and communicate with the wholesale to get more details.

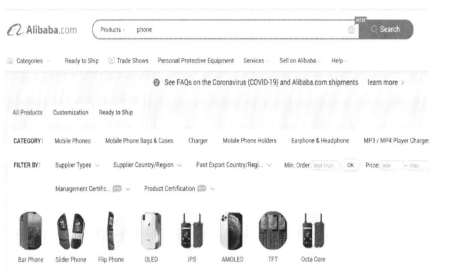

4) What's trade assure?

Alibaba trade assurance protects online orders on Alibaba platform. You may get the money back if you are not satisfied with the product quality after 30 days delivery. Trade assure is free service for buyers. You may choose to order from Trade assure suppliers. If you pay via PayPal or other payment ways that transfers the money directly to the suppliers. Then the Trade assure can't protect your online orders.

5) How can I pay for the product?

There are different payment ways, such as Credit card, Debit card, T/T, West Union, Online Bank Payment etc.

6) Alibaba shipping costs

The shipping cost is quite different when the order quantity varies. You will need to check the exact shipping costs with the supplier.

1) How long does shipping take from china

It really depends on the products you buy and the shipment solution you chose, it would be much quick if ship by Air. Better to contact the seller to get the information. Just give them the quantity you want to order, your address and zip code.

2) Tools for communicating with supplier

You may download an Alibaba App, it's available for both Android and Apple store. You could communicate with the wholesale on the app.

Or you may use webpage to contact the exporter, you will need to sign in first. It's free, and you can sign in with your social media account, Facebook, Google, LinkedIn or Twitter.

Conclusion:

Alibaba is a nice choice if you want to order bulk products export from China to USA or other countries. There are some Chinese trade companies selling on Alibaba.

You already knew how to buy at Alibaba, make sure you check the background of suppliers first, check the factories pictures, the certification etc. Though Alibaba is safe and legit, but there might be some scammers out there. Make sure using the Trade assure and make payment online to protect you from scam on Alibaba.

4.2 AliExpress

1). What's AliExpress? Who owns AliExpress? Where is AliExpress located?

AliExpress is retail platform which was launched in 2010, the owner is Alibaba Group.

You can buy from Chinese customers, including clothing, consumer electronic, watches, shoes etc. A lot of products are free shipping.

2). How to find suppliers?

- Type product keyword into the search bar
- Choose the price range, country, free shipping, free return etc.
- Click on the specific products to check more details or contact the supplier.

Five Tips for finding good supplier:

- Check the store score and years of store. Try to buy from a store has 90 score and more than 3 years on AliExpress.
- Read the reviews of the products, especially the negative reviews.
- Check the price first on 1688 or Taobao, you will know the estimated cost of the product. Don't buy the lowest price with a lot of negative reviews.

- Keep away from the patent products.

3) AliExpress vs Alibaba

- Minimum quantity (MOQ)

AliExpress is retail marketplace, you may buy it one or two pieces.

Alibaba has MOQ, you will need to buy in bulk, for example 100 pieces or 500 pieces.

If you want to buy in bulk, Alibaba would be your choice.

- Shipping cost

Alibaba: The seller uses own logistic carriers. For small quantity, the shipping cost may a little expensive. For large quantity, they can arrange to ship by Sea.

AliExpress: AliExpress is cooperating with different logistic companies, such as 4PX, Yanwen, Post etc. Thus, sellers on AliExpress can get very cheap shipping if they use their service. That's why many products are for free shipping.

- Customized product

Alibaba: You can use your logo or design at a certain quantity. Many factories in china are selling on Alibaba. They provide white label service

AliExpress: Most sellers don't have white label service.

- Drop shipping business / Shopify

If you are doing drop shipping, we strongly recommend you use AliExpress. You don't need to keep any stock, and the AliExpress seller will handle the shipment for you. If you use Oberlo, you may import products from AliExpress to your store directly. Super easy and quick.

4) Is AliExpress legit? Is AliExpress reliable

Yes. AliExpress is absolutely legit and reliable.

5) How to dropship with AliExpress

- Setup your drop shipping store

You may use different solution to build your store, Shopify, Big-Commerce, Mango etc. Create a catchy store for your business.

- Upload the products to your store

You may use a software or hire someone to upload the products for you. Using high-quality images and writing amazing description for your products.

- Order products from AliExpress when you got orders.

You may order products from AliExpress when you received orders. You don't need to keep any inventory.

- AliExpress seller arranges the shipment to your customer.

After you made an order, your supplier will deliver the products directly to your customer.

- You track the orders and finish the order.

Send the order number to your customer, and track the orders till your customer received the product without damage or quality issues.

6) How long does it take to ship from China?

Most suppliers selling on AliExpress use the shipping service offered on AliExpress, such as Ali Standard, Ali economy, Yanwen, epacket etc. The shipment needs about 15-60 days. If you need fast shipping, you may ask the seller to use DHL, FedEx or UPS etc. But you will need to cover the cost.

7)Tools for communicating with supplier

You may download an AliExpress app or use the webpage to contact with the suppliers on AliExpress.

8). Alternatives to AliExpress

There are some other alternatives to AliExpress in China: DH Gate, Lightinthebox, Taobao, 1688 etc.

Conclusion

Both AliExpress and Alibaba belongs to Alibaba group, AliExpress is a quick and easy for you to start drop shipping business at low quantity. When you want bulk buy from China or want to create your own brand, you may consider sourcing from Alibaba.

4.3 DH gate

1). What's Dh gate?

DH gate is an online retail platform, founded in 2004 in Beijing.

2). How to find supplier on DH gate?

If you want to source shoes wholesales in China, type the shoe name. Then choose the minimum order, supplier type.

3). AliExpress VS DH gate

Both AliExpress and DH gate can be a sourcing platform for buying from China. The major difference between them is DH gate can offer discount if you buy in bulk. And MOQ is more than one piece.

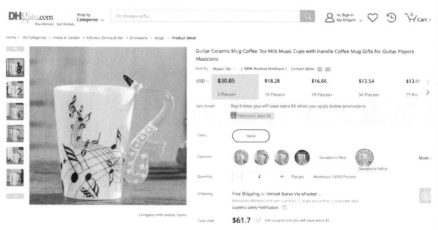

4.4 1688.com

1) What's 1688? Who own 1688?

The 1688.com belongs to Alibaba group, founded in Hangzhou city of China in 2006. It's a B2B wholesale marketplace. This eCommerce platforms offers a wide range of product as Alibaba.

2) Does 1688 have English version?

No, it only has a Chinese version, so you will need to extension to translate it into other language.

3) How to find reliable manufacturer?

Each seller on 1688 has one page which shows the business license, you will need to check the background of the supplier. And each the review of them. Try to select the manufacturers which has more than 5 years of experience on 1688.

4) Can they ship international?

Most of them only ship within Mainland China. Some of them can ship it to other countries.

5) How can you pay the seller?

You may consider use Alipay, Visa, MasterCard/JCB to pay them, or you can ask someone to pay it for you.

6) 1688 VS AliExpress

1688 offers customized products in a low quantity, and you can lower price than AliExpress. We may say that 1688 is the Chinese version of Alibaba.

Due to the language barrier, it will be easier to communicate with suppliers on AliExpress.

4.5 Taobao

1). What's Taobao? Who owns it?

Taobao is a B2C marketplace, founded in 2003 and owned by Alibaba group.

Taobao is one of popular eCommerce platform in China. It has more than 500 million users. The daily active user is more than 60 million.

There are more than 800 million products are selling online. You can find anything you want, no matter a white label product, or you want to find a car part.

2) Can Taobao ship to other countries? And how many days need to ship from China?

Yes. It offers international shipment to these countries, including Canada, USA, Singapore, Japan, Malaysia, Australia, Korea and New Zealand.

Taobao logistic can gather the products your ordered from different stores, then pack them and ship to your address.

Normally, it needs about 14-40 days to ship those countries.

3) How can I pay the seller?

You may use Alipay, Visa, MasterCard/JCB to pay the sellers. The cost is 3% of the amount if you use Visa or MasterCard. If you use Alipay, no extra cost needed.

4) What logistic company do they use to export from China to other countries?

Generally speaking, they use Ali Stand or 4PX to ship internationally.

Conclusion:

Taobao is a great marketplace for importing from China. You may need a translator to contact with the seller when necessary.

4.6 Offline wholesale market

Do you know how many how many provinces are in China?
And are you many wholesale markets in China?

There are 23 provinces in China, and there are more than 50
wholesale markets inside China. Different market has its own
local featured products.

- Yiwu wholesale market

Yiwu wholesale market is one of the popular markets in
China, it's a small community market in Yiwu city,
Zhejiang province. It's built in 1982. It has more than
70,000 stores there. The products cover more than 43
categories, including cosmetic, stationary, textiles, socks
etc.

- Shenzhen Hua Qiang Bei

It's in Shenzhen city of Guangdong province of china. This
market is focus on electronics and components. It contains
11 big electronic market, such as Sag, Saibo, Zhongdian,
HQ-Mart etc.

This market shared more than 50% electronic market in China. This is the center for sourcing electronic products and components.

Know the main market for different product can help sourcing the best suppliers with the best quality.

Summary

We have known the 6 main purchasing channels-- AliExpress, Taobao,1688, DH gate, Alibaba and the wholesale markets in China. Select the right way to source your product and buying from China. We are sure that it will help you find the reliable suppliers for your business.

Chapter 5: Manage your Shopify store

5.1 Fulfillment with Oberlo

If you source products from AliExpress, Oberlo is an excellent tool to help you with fulfillment.

You will need to connect your store with Oberlo first. Here are the processes of fulfillment with Oberlo.

- You got orders from your customers
- Place orders on Oberlo dashboard—manage orders
- Suppliers deliver the products
- Get the track number from AliExpress
- Customers received the orders

Many suppliers offer the same products on AliExpress, you can use the Oberlo to change the supplier. Make sure that you get the best quality with competitive price to get more profit.

You can add multiple suppliers for each product if necessary.

5.2 POD fulfillment

POD means print on demand. When you got orders, you go to the POD platform to place orders, and they will print the design according to your requirements and then ship it.

In terms of the design, you would consider prepare some designs for customers to choose, or your customers can use their own designs.

There are some platforms that provide POD service, such as Printful, Zazzle, Teespring etc. You can choose the sites according to your specific products.

A lot of POD service providers are integrated with Shopify. You can check it on the Shopify app store.

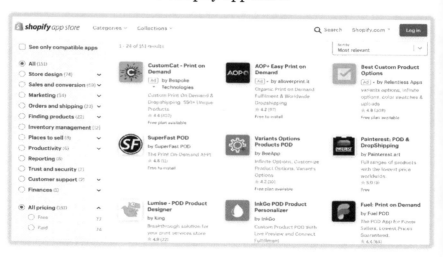

5.3 Warehouse and fulfillment

If you source products from some other countries yourself instead of drop shipping websites. You want to use your own logo and buy it in bulk, you will need to get a warehouse and fulfill the orders.

For example, you source products from China, and you keep your stock in China or your own country. You will need to pack products and arrange the shipment to your customers when you received orders.

There are some advantages for this model:

- Establish your own brand
- You can control the quality and inventory
- You can choose the best suitable way for shipment
- Control the cost.

Chapter 6: Marketing Your Shopify Store

We have successfully created a Shopify store, now it comes the most important part—Marketing your store.

In this chapter, we will show you how to use the following six channels to do marketing:

- Facebook Ads
- Google Ads
- Tiktok marketing
- Email Marketing
- KOL Marketing
- Five Store Branding Tip

6.1 Facebook Ads

Facebook ads can help you precisely target your potential customers. You can use it for selling products and branding.

How to add a Facebook marketing channel on Shopify?

Go to the Shopify Dashboard; choose sales channels, click "+," select "Facebook." You will see the following screenshot. If you have already got a Facebook account, choose the "Connect Facebook account". Otherwise, you will need to sign up for Facebook first.

How to set up ads on Facebook?

Step 1: Create a Facebook business page
You can use your existed Facebook account to create a business account, or you may get a new account to do this.

Create a page, select "Business or Brand", click "Get Started".

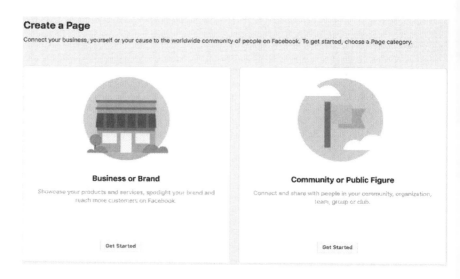

You will need to add your business name or store name. Select the category of your business or your main products. Add the address and phone, then click "Continue".

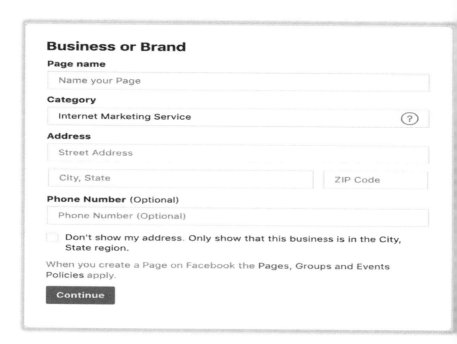

Add a profile picture (or your logo). It is better to use the square image, like 360X360 pixel, 180x 1,80pixel etc. The size of the cover image is 82pixels15 pixel. You can change those images afterward.

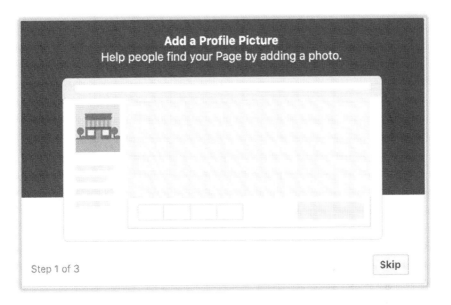

Add a Profile Picture
Help people find your Page by adding a photo.

Step 1 of 3

Skip

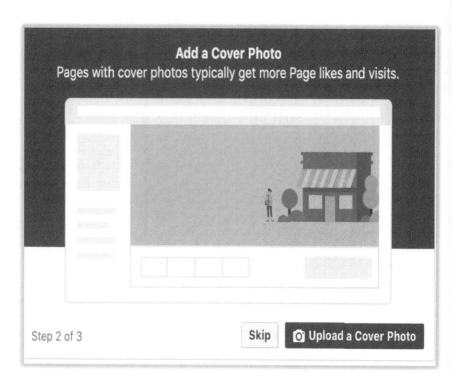

Step 2 of 3

"Add a Button",we may call it the "Call-to-Action button" this is for adding your Shopify URL or other website.

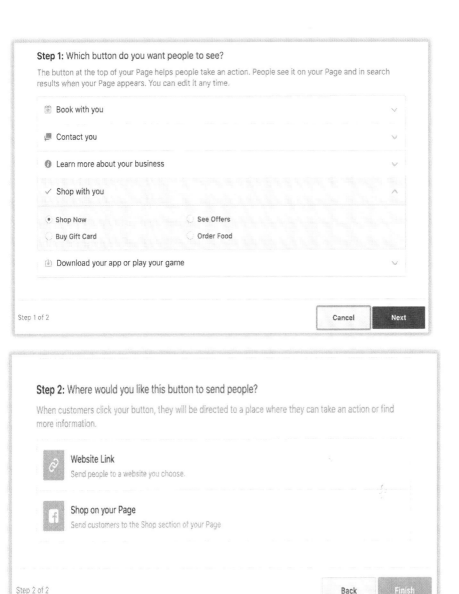

After you finished this, you will need to click n the "setting", to edit the information of your business, such as business description, contact information, location, price, privacy policy, automation greetings etc.

Step 2: Create your ads for your product

How to create Facebook ads?

Go to your Facebook homepage, click the "Promote" on the left side bottom.

Choose your goal for the ads.

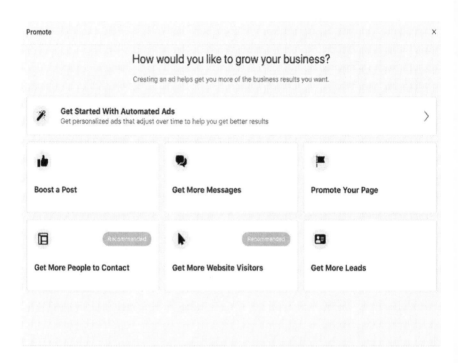

Then name the campaign, set up your target audience, placement, budget, and bidding.

Step 3: Promote your content on Facebook

6.2 Google Ads

Google provides paid advertisements service that was showing in search results, display, or shopping on google.com.

The main benefit of advertising with Google is that you can choose how much you spend, the audience you want to target, and you only pay when someone clicks the ads. It can work faster than search engine optimization, access to comprehensive analytics, and reach more customers.

The cost of Google advertising varies based on many factors, including the competitiveness of your keywords, the industry, your geographic location, the quality of the marketing campaigns, and so on.
The average cost for Google search advertising is $2.30 in the United States. In other countries, the average prices for Google ads are often much lower.

There are mainly three kinds of Google ads for your Shopify store: Search, Display, and Shopping.

Three steps to creating a Google ads account:
1) Get a Gmail account, access to the website :
   ads.google.com
2) Set your campaign

- Budget
- Choose your target audience, including locations, keywords, ads type, etc.

3) Set your bid

How to get ranking on Google?

The Ads position depends on various elements, and you can't buy it directly to the top. We suggest you analyze the keywords you use. High-quality ads and high landing pages are crucial to Google Ads' success.

Landing Page is a webpage to attract people to click to get your marketing goal.

Five Tips for creating a useful Landing Page:

- Get an eye-catching headline
- High-quality image & Design
- Make value
- Social proof
- Call to Action

Keyword research is essential for Google ads. There are a variety of tools for finding related keywords relevant to your post that you may not have noticed. We recommend the two tools: the Google AdWords Keyword Tool and semrush.com. They are great tools that allow you to find keywords related to your topic and spy on the competitors on your niche to see what words and phrases they are using to bring traffic to their websites.

6.3 Tiktok marketing

TikTok is a Chinese video-sharing social networking service owned by ByteDance, a Beijing-based internet technology company founded in 2012. TikTok is ranking on the top 1 on the app store.

TikTok Demographics:

- Device: 52% of TikTok users in the United States are iPhone users.
- Gender: 44% of TikTok users are female, while 56% are male.
- Country: TikTok's geographical use has shown that 43% of new users are from India.
- Age: TikTok has proven to attract the younger generation, as 41% of its users are between the ages of 16 and 24. Among these TikTok users, 90% say they use the app daily.

App downloads: As of May 2020, there are 30 million monthly active users in the United States alone.

6.4 Email Marketing

Email marketing is using email to send a commercial message, typically to a group of people. In a broad sense, every email sent to a potential customer or current consumer could be considered as email marketing. It involves using email to send new product advertisements, request business, or solicit sales or donations.

In this chapter, you will learn the following topics:

Why do we need to choose email marketing?
Do you know how to start making money from emails?
How to monetize email marketing?
How to collect emails for your email marketing?
What are the best tools for email marketing?

- ***Why do we need to need email marketing?***
Email marketing is one of the best practical marketing tools that a small business can invest in. Because email help you reach more mobile consumers, it's instant and convenient. Email marketing can get the highest conversion rates among different marketing tactics. According to the Data & Marketing Association, 66% percent of consumers made an order after receiving a marketing email, and it's easier than social and

direct mail. And transactions from email marketing are three times more profitable than this made on social media, according to the reports from the global management consulting firm McKinsey & Company.

- ***Do you know how to start making money from emails?***

Here are seven proven ways to monetize your email marketing.

- ***How to monetize email marketing?***

1. **Sell Products or services!**

If not, this is your first step. Find a physical product or digital product or service to sell with your email marketing.

- Don't know what to sell by email?

Here is some advice for you to get started:

- Audiobooks and eBooks.
- Training guides.
- Online courses.
- Private virtual coaching.
- Classes or workshops.

2. Sell other people's products or services

When you don't have your own products or services to sell now, you can be an affiliate for other people' s products or services. As an affiliate, you can get commissions from businesses from traffic which convent to sales.

Here's an excellent example of a great affiliate marketing: An online consulting coach offers planning and operations advice to his clients, such as website hosting services, market research, keywords research, landing page design, social media marketing provider — to serve his clients' marketing and sales requirements.

Many companies have different affiliate programs you can join in — like AWeber! You can sign up for our affiliate partner on AWeber.

But before you do the email marketing, make sure you have a good relationship with your subscribers and that you recommend products or services that align with their interests and requirements. Otherwise, they may unsubscribe or delete it directly.

3. Upsell premium or exclusive products

Get bigger orders from your subscribers with an upselling email.

If you're a business coach, your main product is an online monthly membership that includes access to a community of users, and a database of valuable resources—more dollars for a customized coach.

4. Cross-selling & related products

A potential upsells exclusive 1-on-1 coaching sessions. A participant can choose the topic they want you to focus on and ask questions-which they might not feel comfortable asking in a live webinar in a public virtual room filled with other members. Many people are willing to pay

If you are a trainer or consultant, you could offer a free downloadable upper-body worksheet or checklist. If someone wants to request it, they will receive an automated email with the download document— plus an upsell to a comprehensive 6-week program that guarantees the coach results.

Cross-selling is encouraging customers to purchase related or complementary terms. In real life, large businesses usually combine cross-selling and up-selling techniques to increase revenue.

According to the date of the sale, you can identify the products that satisfy your current customers with additional products or services.

You probably have read an email in your inbox right now, "Because you bought this, you might be interested in this, or you are looking for." They sent an email to the online shoppers who get targeted messages based on previous shopping decisions or search result, because they may be more likely to order it again.

Here's an excellent example of a cross-sell:
A digital marketer sells a paid online training course called "How to Become a Master at Google Advertising." Once a person completes the whole course, they're automatically sent an email that cross-sells another course — this time about website design and optimization.

Start sending an automated email with additional recommendations approximately two weeks after a customer's initial order. It's straightforward to set up targeted, automated email sequences by using some email marketing tools, like Mailchimp, ActiveCampaign, etc.

5. Get repeat purchases

Attracting a new customer is 5 to 25 times more expensive than retaining an existing customer. Not only are retention customers cheaper, but also for a long-term profitable business because increasing retention rates by just five percent can increase the profits by 25 to 95 percent.

This method to monetize email marketing works exceptionally well for some businesses that rely on seasonal, recurring goods. For example, a tax manager may email a client at the end of each mind to remind them to prepare for the tax documents.

Getting loyalty schemes is a tried-and-tested method for increasing engagement and get repeat orders.

Reward loyalty

Encourage all your customers to join yours by selling its benefits by email. Whether they'll get exclusive offers, coupons, first views, or free delivery—show them why your loyalty scheme is a must.

6. Have a cart abandonment plan

Sometimes the buyers often get distracted or step away from a purchase because they weren't ready to buy at that moment. You can check the data on your Shopify dashboard.

Now, you can automatically send catchy emails that encouraging them to buy the product they were considering. If your customers received multiple abandoned shopping cart emails, and they will get 2.4 times more to finish the purchase than those who receive only one follow-up email.

You may consider sending the first email in 24 hours, a second email 48 hours after, and possibly a third email around three days of abandonment.

Keep cart abandonment emails short and direct.

You can even offer relevant information to help address questions or concerns they may have or highlight your excellent customer service team.

How to collect emails for your email marketing?
There are a lot of natural methods to build your emails ist for your email marketing. You don't need to buy a list. We will show you how to collect emails both on your website and from other networks.

Using your website to collect emails:

Your website is an excellent place to build an email list.

- Offer freebies on your website, such as checklists, reports, courses, videos, eBooks, Spreadsheets, templates, etc.

- Use popups to different places on your site, triggering the popups after 30 seconds, or after 50% scroll, or triggering popups based on exit intent.
- Promote your newsletter signup throughout your website
- Host online events

Utilizing social media to get emails:

Using social media is an easy way to grow your email list with minimal effort.

Put a signup form on your Facebook fan page, so that anyone visiting your Facebook page can easily subscribe to receive email updates.

o Use Facebook ads

o Run a contest on your social media

o Ask Twitter followers to share your content.

o Create your own channel on a platform like YouTube or Pinterest, podcast, or other networks, then links back to your site.

- **What are the best tools for email marketing?**

There are a lot of email marketing tools you can choose. You can use the tools with no tech and design background. Here we are recommending two free tools and two paid tools.

Two free tools: **MailChimp & SendinBlue**

Mailchimp features

Mailchimp is one of the most fantastic email marketing tools. It offers a free plan up to 2,0000 contacts. You can choose the free plan when to get started with a limited budget. The paid plan starts at $9.99 per month, up to 50,000 contacts. You can update the plan when you need it.

Here are the key features of MailChimp:

- 1 click automation
- Marketing CRM (Customer Relationship Management)
- Visual email builder
- Email templates and layouts
- Contact management tools
- Basic / Detailed report
- Marketing channels: Facebook & Instagram Ads, Google Ads.
- Behavioral targeting

Sendinblue

Sendinblue provides a free plan, and you can send up to 300 emails per day, unlimited contacts. It's an excellent choice to start with Sendinblue.

Sendinblue paid plan starts at $25 per month.

Key features:

- Visually design your email with drag-and-drop
- Email templates library
- SMS marketing
- A/B testing
- Unlimited contacts & details
- Customizable signup forms
- Sales CRM (Customer Relationship Management)
- Integrated with Facebook Ads

Two paid tools: **ActiveCampaign & Constant Contact**

ActiveCampaign: the paid plan starts at $9 per month with unlimited sending, up to 3 users.

Key features:

- Subscription forms
- Site Tracking
- Facebook custom audiences
- SMS
- Gmail Extension for Chrome
- Advanced reporting
- IOS CRM App

Constant Contact: the plan starts at $20 per month. The first month is free.

Key features:

- Unlimited emails
- Customizable templates
- Tracking & reporting
- Google Ads
- Facebook & Instagram Ads & Insights
- Ecommerce Marketing Basic

Conclusion: using one of the email marketing tools make your work more effective and grows more.

6.5 KOL Marketing

KOL means A key opinion leader, also called an influencer, is a member of a community or social media whose expert advice is respected by others in their field. Key opinion leaders are authorities on a specific topic; they usually have a targeted audience specific to their niche.

Brands collaborate with KOLs to:

- Reach more people in a target market

- Gain credibility through word-of-mouth marketing from a trusted expert

There are some platforms that you can research and identify KOL for your store:

- Buzzsumo
- Followerwonk
- Upfluence

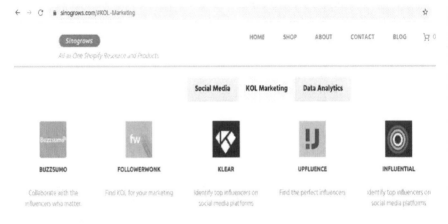

6.6 Store Branding Tips

A good brand can help you stand out from your competitors and get more profit.

Here are five tips for establishing your branding:

First: Create a brand identity, including business name, logo, slogan, brand color, font, product images, packages, customized theme, etc. All these factors will build a strong brand for your business.

Second: Reach your target audience on social media, such as Facebook, Instagram, Tiktok etc.

Third: Focus on product quality; quality is one of the most important things. It helps to maintain your customers' satisfaction and loyalty.

Forth: Build good relations with your suppliers. Make sure the supply chain works effectively.

Fifth: Create different formats of your products, including images, videos, graphs, etc. Videos are becoming more and more popular. Creating product demo videos and explainer videos can catch more attention from your customers.

Conclusion

We learn some marketing channels in this book. But there are a lot of networks that you may use for marketing, such as Instagram, Youtube, Snapchat, Quora, etc.

We recommend you choose the best marketing channel for your Shopify business.
Different budget and products may have different channels for marketing.

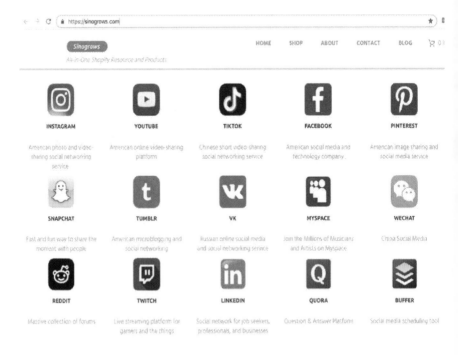

Chapter 7: SEO Shopify store

stands for search engine optimization is the process of growing
the quality and quantity of website traffic by increasing
the visibility of a website on search engines. SEO refers to the
improvement of unpaid results (known as "natural" or
"organic" results) and excludes direct traffic and the purchase
of paid placement. Additionally, it may target different kinds
of searches, including image search, video search, academic
search news search, and industry-specific vertical
search engines. Promoting a site to increase the number
of backlinks, or inbound links, is another SEO tactic.

In this chapter, we will learn how to do on-site optimization
and off-site optimization, also we will recommend some
Shopify SEO apps and tools.

7.1 How to do On-Site Optimization

One of the most critical methods you can use to achieve higher
rankings in the results of a search engine is on-page SEO. A

website is the focus of all SEO processes and if it is not properly optimized for both search engines and users, your chances of getting traffic from search engines will be minimized. On-page SEO or on-site SEO, is the method of optimizing a web page's structure and content. On-page SEO's ultimate goal is to speak the language of search engines' and help search engine crawlers understand the meaning and context of your web pages. It is important because it provides a number of signals to search engines to help them understand the meaning of your content.

Search engines tend to connect web pages with keywords and search terms users type in the search box during the indexing and ranking processes. You can guide them through on-page SEO elements as to which keywords you want to rank your pages. It is also called' on-page' because any changes made to the optimization of a webpage contribute to improved user experience. Therefore, on-site SEO is a subset of SEO.

Moving forward, here is a list of all SEO strategies on-page:

- Publish high-quality content
- Optimize page titles and meta descriptions
- Optimize page content
- Headings and content formatting
- SEO photos and other visual elements
- URL optimization
- Internal links

- External links
- Page loading speed
- App friendliness
- Feedback and on-page SEO

Publish High-Quality Content

With SEO or without SEO, a website with bad content will not succeed. With SEO, a website with good content can get even better!

So, what's a good content!

· Original content

Text, images, photos, presentations, info-graphics and comments, etc., on your website, should not be copied or rewritten.

· Exclusive content for your website

If it's your own content, it's not good for your site if you've already published it on another website.

· Text element content

Write text to accompany your non-text content. When you post videos on your website, for example, try to add a summary text as well. Try to describe with words what the picture is all about if you add pictures.

· Useful material

Don't publish content for publishing purposes. Make sure that what goes live, it always adds value to your website and readers before hitting the publish button.

· Well-researched content

Viewers don't want to read quick prepared posts, nor do search engines.

· Unbiased material

Make sure that what you write is unbiased and covers all sides of a story if you write about a particular topic or answer a question.

Optimize Page Titles and Meta Descriptions

When your pages are read by search engines, they check the page title and page description, among other things.

We do so because they need to understand what the page is all about and then place the page in a position in their index based on other criteria (off-page SEO, domain authority, competition, etc.).

Every page must have a unique title to help both search engines and users understand the purpose of the website.

Page Title Optimization Tips

Apply keywords to the page title start, apply the goal keywords to the page title start where necessary. It lets search engines understand from the outset what the page's targeting keywords are.

That doesn't mean you should go through the line and start stuffing keywords. If at the beginning you can't have a keyword, it's not the end of the world. Only make sure that the title is part of your goal keyword.

Write Short and Concise Titles

It doesn't have to be a very long page title. The normal recommendation is to keep it below 55 characters as this is the maximum number of characters shown in the search results by Google.

Include Numbers and Power Words

Including numbers in the title as well as power words like "Perfect, actionable, incredible, checklist, etc." allows titles more relevant and this enhances their "Click-Through-Rate".

You don't need to Include your Domain in the Title

You don't have to include your domain name in the title because it's automatically added by Google. The 60 characters can be used to provide a precise description of the website.

An exception to the concerned rule is when you have a popular brand that can be easily recognized by people, in this situation you can find the title of your domain.

The definition of the website is what the searcher will see on the results page of the search engine (SERPS). For each page, it must be concise, up to 200 characters special. It's your chance to advertise your page and persuade people not to pick one of the other links, but to click on your button and visit your website. It is note able that Google does not always show the given Meta description, but if they feel it is more helpful to the searcher, they use an automated description several times.

Meta Description Optimization Tips

Although Google may not use your description, avoiding using auto-generated descriptions that sometimes make no sense is always a best practice. Add your target keyword(s) in the description—Google still highlights the search terms in both the title and description so adding your target keywords makes descriptions more relevant and appealing to the searcher.

Optimize Page Content

Content SEO is part of the on-page SEO and has to do with optimizing the target keywords ' actual content. The very first step is to do your keyword search before posting a piece of content (whether it's text, pictures, audio or video). This is necessary in order to find out what search terms users type in the search box and create content that can serve their intent. Once you have selected your target keywords, you can create a list of related keywords (also known as LSI keywords), long-tail keywords and use them in your names, explanations, headings and content on the website.

Why? Because Google search algorithms have become more intelligent with the introduction of Rank Brain, and they are also looking for topic relevance in addition to keyword relevance in content. This means you need to supplement your content with LSI keywords to make your content more applicable to broad topics.

There are various ways to determine which keywords are considered relevant to your target keywords by Google. The easiest and quickest way is to take advantage of Google's three features: Google's suggestion, people's request, and related searches.

Headings and Content Formatting

A page needs to be formatted properly. Think of it as a report needing heading (h1) and subheadings (h2, h3).

The H1 Tag Every page requires a single H1 tag. If you use WordPress, the title of a page will be covered in H1 tags by default.

You can always choose to have the same tag < title > and < h1 > or provide the heading with an alternative title.

Note that search engines display what they find in the tag of the title and not the tag of h1 in the test. There are situations where you want to differentiate between the two, such as the example below: As far as the other headings are concerned (h2, h3), the things you need to keep in mind are the following:

- Do not use a single word for a heading, but make your headings interesting and useful for users who like skim reading an article.
- Hierarchically use headings i.e. the first heading tag is < h1 > and then < h2 > and then < h3 >, < h4 > etc.
- Subheadings are a great place to use similar keywords in your material.

Formatting content don't just throw text on a page, but make sure it's readable.

Using bold, emphasized or italics to highlight key parts of a page.

- Use a decent font size (minimum 14px).
- Split the text into small sections (max 3-4 lines).
- Using ample spacing to make the text easier to read between the paragraphs.

- Use CSS to create distinguishing sections and divide the text into smaller, more manageable sections.

SEO Photos and other Visual Elements

Images and other multimedia elements Images are important. They make a website easier to understand and more interesting. The biggest image problem is that search engines don't understand them and contribute to a page's loading speed. Best SEO image management techniques.

• Using original images.

You need to reference the source if you need to use an existing image from the site.

• Optimize the image size

The smaller the image size (in bytes) the better.

• Use the ALT tag to describe the image

Which helps search engines understand the meaning of the image.

• Use descriptive filenames

Try to use descriptive filenames, such as' man-doing-push-ups.jpg' and not just name your image' image1.jpg.'

• Use a Content Delivery Network

If you have a lot of pictures on a single page, you can use a CDN service to load the page faster. Simply put, a variety of servers can host and serve your images, which speeds up the loading process.

URL Optimization

It is critical for maximum SEO to optimize your URLs. There are two pieces to it. The first part is optimizing the URL and the second part is the structure of the URL. A permanent connection (also referred to as a slug) is each page's unique URL. Effective URLs should be less than 255 characters and use hyphens to distinguish the various parts from each other. Like the page title, a simple, succinct SEO-friendly URL contains the target keyword.

URL Structure

The structure of the URL will mimic the real website configuration.

Make use of Categories

Organize the pages into groups to help users and search engines find what they want faster.

It's like getting a warehouse with loads of uncategorized items as opposed to a warehouse with all the items allocated to a specific category.

Internal Links

Linking to sites on your website is very relevant to SEO because it's like creating your own website. The first step that a search engine spider can take once a page has been discovered is to follow the links on that page (both internal and external). So, when they land on your website, they'll read your page and go if you don't have any other links in the text.

If you have links to other sites on your website, these will also be taken into consideration.

When explained above when search engines find a page with links, they will also go and read those pages, so you can use this method to inform search engines about your website pages that they have not yet found.

It's another way to tell search engines which are the most valuable pages. Every website has some more important pages than others. External links are one of the ways to identify the most relevant pages by submitting more external links to them.

It's a way to increase users spend on your site. A user who reads your post is more likely to click on a link to read more about a particular topic, thereby increasing both the time spent on your site, the number of pages per visit, and the bounce rate.

- Do not use keywords only for your internal links • Use internal links when they are useful to your user
- Not more than 15 internal links per page (this is my opinion and not based on any analysis or study)
- Provide links to the main body of your website (not in the footer or sidebar) if necessary

External Links

Most webmasters are afraid to connect to other websites after the introduction of Panda and Penguin. We think this will cause an issue for Google, but that's incorrect.

By linking to other websites related to high quality, you increase your content's trustworthiness and this is good for SEO.

Google can also use external links to help you understand the subjects that you address in your posts.

Page Loading Speed

Two increasingly important SEO strategies are "Speed" and "mobile-friendliness".

Google is spending an enormous amount of money to make the site quicker. Someone will speak in every Google about the importance of speed and their ability to include the fastest websites in their index.

They also officially added speed as one of the established ranking criteria to' push' website owners to take speed into account.

Therefore, we know for sure that when it comes to SEO and ranking, website pace matters.

As a webmaster, your job is to ensure that your website loads by considering the recommendations of Google as quickly as possible. It is not only perfect for SEO to have fast-loading websites, but also for customer retention and conversions.

App Friendliness

Today almost 60 percent of Google's searches come from mobile devices. It means you are already losing half of the future traffic if your website is not mobile-friendly.

What are you going to do!

Make sure your website is mobile-friendly as a first move. Use Google's mobile friendly tool to check your website and fix any critical issues.

Then take one step further and check your website on your mobile, as a real user would, and make sure that everything, including your CTA buttons, is displayed correctly.

There's nothing to think about mobile-friendliness on general websites with responsive design.

Feedback and On-Page SEO

Most people believe that comments are no longer important with the rise of social media sites, but they are wrong.

Observations on the blog are still relevant. It's an indicator, as Google's Gary Illyes said, that people like your content and connect with the website, and this can really improve your SEO.

Users will most likely read the existing comments before posting a new comment, and this is another way to increase the amount of time they spend on the page and your website.

- Always moderate comments before publishing
- Avoid posting comments that are too generic
- Only accept comments that are important to the content of the page and add value

- Do not approve comments where users do not use a real name
- Always respond to comments, this will encourage more people to comment.

Moreover, you need both off-page SEO and on-page SEO to achieve maximum visibility in the search engines and to keep your users happy.

On-page SEO is more important for new websites, at least. It speaks' the language of search engines It makes more sense to start with on-page SEO and get it right instead of trying to persuade search engines to give you better off-page SEO rankings. Search engines are computer programs (software) that don't' see' a website like a regular person, but they can only understand code and the HTML language in particular. You're' sing' their language with SEO and particularly on-page SEO. Your goal is to help them understand what a page is all about by giving them different signals through a page structure and content optimization. The through the chances of achieving better rankings are the more signs you will give them.

On-Page SEO is also about the customer. Never forget that your primary objective is to make the users pleased. Off page SEO can bring people to the website, but the results will be disappointing if it is not set up properly or if it is not user-friendly. It's incredible, but it's real that most websites are not designed for search engines today.

Given the abundance of SEO knowledge, many website owners believe it's not worth trying SEO and they're leaving before they start. On-page SEO has too much to offer in both usability and traffic for these situations. It is sometimes all you need if you run a small business website and you need local customers to search for different terms on Google, then on-Page SEO is all you might need to do.

Off-page SEO comes after On-Page SEO You need to make sure it is optimized and in good condition before you even start thinking about how you can promote your website.

So, dealing with on-site SEO is the first step and then moving to off-site SEO.

7.2 How to do Off-Site Optimization

What is **off-site** SEO?

"**Off-page** SEO" (also called "**off-site** SEO") refers to actions taken outside of your own website to impact your rankings within **search engine** results pages

There are two important factors for off-site optimization: Backlinks and social media marketing.

Backlinks are links from other website links to your website. It means you get "votes" from other websites. It will help you boost your ranking on search engines.

Social media marketing means using **social media** networks to connect with your audience to build your brand, increase sales, and drive **website** traffic.

Recommended Tools for SEO

1) Google Analytics

It's free to sign up for a Google Analytics account and it's fast and easy. You can use the Google account to sign into the web browser's Google Analytics. You can go to google.com to check for data from Google. Users need to add new analytics account after signing in and then add new property to start using analytics tools from Google.

There are five main features that make Google Analytics Tools a remarkable useful tool:

- Goals
- Statistics tracking, including Revenue, Acquisition, Inquiry and Engagement etc.
- Integration of Ad-Words
- Management of campaigns through URL Builder
- Tracking of e-commerce

2) Google Search Console

Google Search Console is also a free tool, which Google offers to help website owner's track and manage Google Search results for their website. This warns you when pages on your website cannot be crawled and indexed by Google. You, also, may have helpful tips on how to fix the errors in the crawl.

3) SEMrush

SEMrush is one of the best SEO software's on the market. It provides a comprehensive set of tools to maximize the traffic. To find organic keywords and search terms you can quickly rate with, you can use it. It also allows you to do some research and see your competitors' keywords and how to beat them.

SEMrush SEO Writing Assistant tool lets you boost the quality of your website to beat your target keyword's top 10 rankings.

7.3 Shopify App: Plug in SEO

This is a Shopify app, free plan available for this app. You don't need to do any code, it will help you easier ways to optimize SEO ranking of your Shopify Store. You can edit the headings tags, description etc.

Conclusion

You have made it to the end of *Shopify Guide 2020* .

We hope you can know the whole process of creating a money-making Shopify store, and know the tools you want to do research ,manage store, marketing products, branding and affiliate marketing.

Hope this book can inspire you think differently about making money from Shopify. The industry is constantly shifting. Keep learning, testing and improving.

Happy Shopify Business!

JESSICA KER

Here is our All-in-One Free Resource for Shopify business. Please check our website: www.sinogrows.com

If you have any questions, you can reach out us on Facebook group.
https://www.facebook.com/groups/65025056553013 0/

Bonus:Checklist for Creating & Launching a Shopify Store

1. Getting Started

- ☐ Choose a profitable niche
- ☐ Sourcing suppliers and products
- ☐ Your store name
- ☐ Your logo
- ☐ Bank card & PayPal account
- ☐ Email address for signing up on Shopify
- ☐ A mindset that you will be successful

2. Create a Shopify store

- ☐ Sign up for Shopify
- ☐ Name your store
- ☐ Understand the Shopify panel
- ☐ Get a domain & email under your domain
- ☐ Install the theme

- ☐ Create main menu, footer & pages

- ☐ Change the logo, banner

- ☐ Create a track order page "Return Policy", "Term of Service", "Privacy Policy" and "Shipping policy"

- ☐ Upload products, picture, price, inventory, shipping methods, trust badges

- ☐ Set Email newsletter

3. Setting, Payment, Plan & Tools

- ☐ Choose a Shopify Plan

- ☐ Set up your payment gateway

- ☐ Test your track order page, subscribe

- ☐ Test "add to cart & checkout page "

- ☐ Install Google analytics and Google search console

- ☐ Make plan for marketing

- ☐ Site speed test

- ☐ Website SEO

Reference

https://en.wikipedia.org/wiki/Search_engine_optimization

https://ecommercefastlane.com/7-ways-to-build-a-shopify-ecommerce-brand-that-matters/

https://graphicmama.com/blog/stong-brand-visual-identity/

https://smallbusiness.chron.com/quality-important-business-57470.html

https://www.activecampaign.com/blog/key-opinion-leaders

https://en.wikipedia.org/wiki/TikTok

https://mediakix.com/blog/top-tik-tok-statistics-demographics/

https://www.businessinsider.com/tiktok-marketing-trends-predictions-2020

https://blog.hootsuite.com/tiktok-stats/

https://www.statista.com/topics/871/online-shopping/

https://www.liquidweb.com/woocommerce-resource/best-dropshipping-products/

https://alidropship.com/how-to-find-a-niche-market-for-dropshipping-store/

https://dodropshipping.com/products-to-avoid-dropshipping/

https://www.entrepreneurbusinessblog.com/blog/2019/10/14/worst-dropshipping-niches-why/

https://www.bigcommerce.com/blog/amazon-statistics/

Printed in Great Britain
by Amazon

49817022R00078